COMMENTARY

Jock Stein

British Library Cataloguing in Publication Data:

a catalogue record for this publication

is available from the British Library

ISBN   978-1-912052-40-0

© Handsel Press 2017

Typeset in 11.5pt Palatino Linotype at Haddington,
Scotland

Printed by West Port Print & Design, St Andrews

Poetry Series Logo designed by Graeme Clark

Contents

Ancient poets *"shaped* and established reality and truth"

Tomas Sedlacek, *Economics of Good and Evil*,
Oxford 2011, 94

"In poetry the language itself is present to us . . . a living something that allows us to move through it and beyond . . ."

Iain McGilchrist, *The Master and his Emissary*,
Yale 2009, 184

War Talk

Language is kinder than reality, well
meaning, highbrow stuff. Words tell
our eyebrows to relax, they bend our ears
and calm our fears with logic out of hell.

So friendly fire has only good intentions,
if taking out a person by mistake
is just some virtual target practice.
Smart bombs are really clever, they
must demonstrate such sincere skill
to make a kill that's clean, and peer
reviewed by military intelligence.

I.E.D.s are economical with language
and with truth, if 'improvised' suggests
it may not work this time around. Sheer
damage must be totally excused
by multiplying syllables till they spell
col-lat-er-al – well, to make an omelette
you need to break some eggs –
and what are eggs but tiny shells
in which the future of a species dwells?

Tax Haven

Guernsey

Colours fight. All smiles at first,
they decorate lagoons on Renoir's coast,
silken foil round jagged rocks. Above
the cliffs each mansion wraps its green
around itself and leaves the turquoise sea
to show the shifty side of human skin:
eternal blue, or with a swirl of jealousy
embracing gold within our veins?
Eco-green? No, ego-green, owner-occupying
high grounds of finance, while down below
the poison blackballs old sea-lanes of trust.
We tread on bluebells, though they know
that every colour has its seasons,
and every island has its reasons.

Refugee Status

The apples lie unburied in the grass;
one side is green, the other red,
but colours fade when you are dead
and lying at sea level.

The waves delivered Alan to the shore;
his skin was dark, and mine is light,
but colours fade when you take flight
and end up at sea level.

The Parties wait, uncertain in the main,
one brand is red, another blue,
but colours fade when you are through
with lying at sea level.

So pick the fruit, unblemished, while you can,
one side is red, another green,
but colours fade once you have seen
we're equal at sea level.

*Note: the extended family of Aylan Kurdi have asked that in
English his name be given as Alan.*

Two Bronzed Men

David Hume

His home swallowed by the makeover
of St Andrew Square, Davy Hume
has taken refuge on a High St plinth,
his wavy hair in green tinged bronze:
great excoriator of religious rot,
bare-chested, as befits a philosopher
determined to pare the apples
of conventional thought down
to the core, and spit the pips
at prejudice.
               Upon his knee
he balances a stony reputation,
labelled by some wag "a good book
has no ending", flagging up
a dialogue still pending with more
than natural theology.

Adam Smith

He thought well. He meant well. He lived well.
He deserves this statue by the City Chambers
to the author of *The Wealth of Nations*.

Is he not the father of free enterprise?
He has earned this jacket with eleven buttons,
this cloak, this curled wig, this reputation.

Now his eyes and lips are bronze, to match
the hearts of those who cherry-pick his writings,
leaving out his checks and balances to power.

On the Runway

Crane fly challenging the breeze
alights, a tiny airship
on a paper runway. Six knees

genuflect upon a waiting clip
board, asking us to look
beyond a random insect trip

to what is stirring in the book
of Scotland's history, which we
are writing, questioning this fluke

of time which lets us see
so many possibilities, behind
September's serious apogee

of yes or no. I find
this fragile daddy longlegs
focuses the national mind

which flits between the dregs
of fear and sheer mis-selling
of the arguments. It begs

the issue, which is spelling
out in song and story who we are
and want to be: not telling

one another we'll be far
more wealthy if we choose
this way or that. The bar

must rise, so that we lose
our fatal lust for things
that rust and die, refuse

the lies, hold truth which
  brings
us hope, and trust that sees

our lift off come on gentle
  wings.

In May 2014, a 'Bus Party' of leading Scottish writers and folk musicians spent a week touring Scotland, performing and chatting with people about their hopes for a better Scotland in the context of the forthcoming Referendum. A support group handled transport and finance.

This terza rima *poem was written at Stromness in Orkney, when a crane fly came and perched on my clip board . . .*

Shock and Awe

Shock is not a stranger.
          It comes for you at night, in the early hours,
              strips you defenceless;
        it is electric, tortured, ruthless,
              sometimes terminal.
Shock travels
        in the packs of refugees, on the backs
              of Libyan and Syrian
        with the guns of IS and the policies
              of better states.
        It kick the brains of Europe,
              changes a regime.
Shock is hardly new.
          Seven hundred years ago
        they crept down through Balquhiderock wood,
              in the early hours,
        while the English slept off their carousing.
          Out across the Carse
        they marched, to park their pikes with Bruce
              in front of Edward's camp.
      The Earl of Gloucester saw the danger –
             too late he charged
             and fell. Ill omen
             for the rebel foxhunt,
             Scots too close,
        the English cavalry and archers stymied.
      Edward fled,
          carried shock waves down to Berwick
          far beyond the Bannock Burn.

Shock is clever.

50 years ago, a certain Milton Friedman
spotted ECT in Canada,
and modelled for the CIA a perfect storm
to paralyse a generous economy
(think Indonesia and Chile),
tweak the economic brains
and ready them for Western enterprise.

Occasionally
failure is rather public
(think Iraq: shock and awe
now shock and raw
behaviour in Islamic State).

Shock is natural.

Earthquakes multiply, and when the Asian giant tsunami
flooded villages,
tore apart communities,
the tourist lure made governments prevent them
from rebuilding as they chose.

Shock is here to stay.

But don't get used to it.

Fight back with care   and great intelligence.

Guard those early hours.

Exegete your history   your land   your culture.

Let humour clean, not soil your memories.

Build good relationships.

Hold legal pistols at the heads of rulers.

Nourish all your faith   your hope   your love.

Cloudy Skies

Signs of the times they used to be: yet
now quite tamed by weather forecasters
who phrase and frame even disasters
with such words as 'butterfly effect'.

Tonight four skies are forming a new front,
tonight the Brexit backward blast
has messed up every other forecast,
turned our long-term weather back to front.

So cumulus is threatening streaks of cirrus,
nimbus gathers close to a mackerel sky;
they're fishy times indeed – who casts a fly
without a sense of what may rise for us?

Unsettled

Hard it is to leave your country
die at sea like Alan Kurdi
live in exile as Malala does
feel an AK47 in your back
stand by the barbed wire
know there are landmines
exploding in your heart.

You should get out more, they said
but I am exhausted by survival
all other energy vacuumed
into the black hole of my past
history flattened by officialdom
my future crushed into a cage
and crying bleak goodbyes.

Eurocost

for Michaela Gheorghe, at Gavinana

At Sunday noon in Tuscany the church bells ring
for younger generations lost in far-off jobs
who come again to resurrect the villages.
Who scattered them? The EU and its discipline
which closed an industry and changed a way of life.
Or was it just bad management?
Or is it economic destiny, is progress
programmed in some raw collective gene,
triggered by the alcohol within the banking system?
Is 'made in China' label for disease
or showcase for a friendly escalator
taking us to dig for gold on Mars
and base our manufacture on the Moon?

At Sunday noon in Tuscany the church bells ring.
At Monday noon in Germany Merkel is king
– or queen, but such a difference is lost
among the larger things the Euro cost.

Referendum

Our types are chosen: Ayrshire bard, Aberdeen
oilman, Ettrick shepherd, Falkirk bairn
for me, and maybe just a touch of Allan
Ramsay: "On this brae I crack with kings."

"Whit's for ye'll no go past ye." Is that saw
our closest call with providence? What about
the Darien disaster, or the Royal Bank,
did they just happen? Are we dust or fleas
on Satan's hoof or can we claw back
some humanity, and choose with courage?
Who am I? What values cross my path, or
cross my palm and lead me to the dark side?

Give me mongrel strength. No bigsy breeding,
no wracked, cracked genes, feeding cringe
or needing binge of drunken make believe.
If we have myths, let them be kind and true,
to make us song and symbol, right and wrong,
so we can live and die for something strong.

Cloud and Fire

Surreal winter cloudscape, three times layered
along the Ochils, cradling Sherriffmuir
as if to gentle history, and make
an overture in art to things impossible.

Take time and outstretched fingers, run them
carefully along those bars of fog, soft striped
dawnwear for the hills which know the time
to sleep, and wake when Spring unfolds, to
do the duty of each season; or maybe
veils, concealing futures languishing
in jails, unvisited since unimagined?
What season now for Scotland, what videotype
of land is waiting to be brought to birth?
Stylish, connected, rich in mind – or just unkind?

What poet politician is there who will dare
lift off the blindfolds we all wear
and speak the words we cannot say?
What fire by night will match the cloud by day?

Wealthy Nation

Left and Right: two feet that kick their targets
wealth and poverty, sloganning a nation stuck
in apathy, despair or affluent ipaddery
(offering mirages and their virtual riches) –
depending where and when you push your luck
as poet, commentator or observant citizen.
Light twitterers and heavy letter writers
plunge their virtual pens into the ruck,
cherry picking Adam Smith or Robert Burns,
citing innovators, quoting wise and foolish,
whether Kerevan or Fry or even Friar Tuck
who, remember, had a fairly moral take
on wealth, as did the great economist
so glibly mentioned out of context. Muck
and brass no longer meld: *that* Scotland
saw its coal and steel and heavy jobs
that built great merchant houses come unstuck
and leave us vulnerable. No single vision
grips the minds and heads of those who,
losing God, can only blindly pass the buck
to lesser characters like May or Sturgeon.
Come back, true poverty of spirit, offering us
a wealth of wisdom which will never duck
the questions we should put to Left and Right.

Making the Cut

Did the tree feel it? Did anyone notice
that top un-treed, cut and laid out on the grass
to challenge urban planning, withering
the hopes of anyone resolved to plant
some beauty at the city's heart?

And did she feel it? Did anyone notice
that girl upended, cut and made just like her ma's
been since her teens, another bloody scalp
for torturers who want to prove you can't
keep beauty in a child-like heart.

Jihad

Jihad, scary word: yet beautiful to Nasser
and Reyaad, hating usury and vice
so celebrated daily in our media,
and ready to fight for something better.
Before we shake our heads, condemn
those militants out of hand, and
settle back into our Western ways,
let's ask ourselves whose fault it is
that those so quickly radicalised
have not been nourished in a deeper
jihad, rooted in the way of love,
not iron-fisted in religious glove.

Lost Civilisation

The Book of Lamentations

A litany of death connects the world,
disaster joins the poetry of then and now;
and while we gag and find tears prick
our eyes, the fire keeps running,
overtaking people, history and culture,
burning like the anger of a god.

"That's it!" some cry, "The vengeance of a God
ignored and slighted: all across the world
it's blasphemy and pornographic culture
that is thriving, driving our affairs. Now
listen to the revelation; hear the running
feet, feel the terror and the sword prick!"

"Primitive! Our god is education. Prick
that ancient bubble of belief in God.
Learn from westerners just how to run
a modern democratic state; world
affairs are our responsibility. Now
you have the chance, renew your culture!"

So the bombs and bullets fly. A culture
dies, heads roll, and no-one's prick
or pussy's torture-proof, for now
the ancient laws are gone; that god
indeed is dead, and all the world
is mad; marauders make the running.

Tragedy and tears just keep on running
as two enemies collude to make a culture
bloody hell. Just what in all the world
will change the grisly game, and prick
the conscience of the blind, find a God
of mercy, halt the slaughter here and now?

The Middle East's a cockpit, then and now.
It shows us human sin and sorrow, running
through its history, and bumping into God
who wears them, bears them in the culture
of a seed that grew to let God prick
out bold a seedling hope for all the world.

Lament is there to prick the tumours
of the world's despair, to hold a culture
running out of time. Now, where is God?

Macro-economic Forecasting

"It was to avoid the historic British problem – the violence of the repeated boom and bust cycles of the past – that we established the new monetary framework based on consistent rules: the symmetrical inflation target; settled well understood procedures – Bank [of England] independence, and openness and transparency."

Gordon Brown addressing the British Chamber of Commerce national conference, April 5th 2000

Ask Xenophon, the first economist,
when to plant your crops: he will say,
"I know my limitations".
Ask Xenophon, citizen of Athens,
when to go to war: he will tell you,
"Go to Delphi, ask
the Oracle to predict State revenue."
Poets were the ones who spelt the truth
of cereals and credit.

Ask Pharaoh how to run a surplus:
he will say, "I dreamt of cows and corn,
and with a little help
from my first minister, ex Hebrew slave,
I set our tax at twenty full per cent
for seven golden years.
Prophets make quite good economists
in lean times too, I came to think
– austerity made me rich."

Ask the Matrix Oracle for advice:
it's still that delphic "Neo, know thyself".
As Government Adviser,
you might profit by her wisdom,
leave politicos to call elections,
hazard boom or bust.
Pollsters love the chance to forecast
people's choices. Poets write their words
as if it matters.

"It is time to start calling Quantitative Easing what it is: a hidden tax on the wealth of middle-class savers and pensioners which, on the one hand, the government can use to finance the deficits associated with a large, modern welfare state and, on the other, redistribute wealth to the top 5% of households. That is not only monetary policy. It is fiscal policy, which the Bank [of England] has de facto *taken over."*

Guardian, 28/9/2016

The Odds Against

1 Love

Three flags fly on every writer's roundabout:
they're honour, passion, unrequited love
– with human tragedy just one remove
away from bliss. The cynics can dine out
on disappointment, salt their appetites
with Sturgeon, wager on who'll eat their hat,
and wonder whether May be this or that.
A poet eats the hurt of broken rites,
drains the dregs of loss. Like running water,
words oxygenate a stagnant pond,
give empty caves a hint of life beyond,
soften scars of misery, clear disorder.

Flag it up: contemporary or past,
some fool will pull it half way down the mast.

2 Talent

gift
buffed
chuffed
lift

cuffed
sniffed
miffed
stuffed

adrift
rebuffed
snuffed
makeshift

left
bereft

3 Money (a Spanish painting: '*Oro*')

His tongue is taut, his eyeballs shake,
his tendons stretch, his fingers stab
with frozen lust, a greedy grab
at gold the man will never make:
his hands and arms one ghastly knot
that ties a people, keeps their eyes
glued to a ghastly insect, size
of scorpio, shape of pound sign, pot
of gold beneath a fairy bow
that tempts and teases, mocks and lies,
arches eyebrows of the wise
who know that life just isn't so.

Hernández stabs his palette knife
into the flesh of human life.

4 Politics

Flit from Catalonia,
think of this:
the stale piss
exhaling ammonia
from referenda
gone amiss,
antithesis
of hopes to mend a
broken Britain
with some clear
steps out of fear.

But that's not on
for Scotland, England
now in bingo land.

5 Faith

Talent scouts are always looking out
for promise, plumping on some weary horse
who has a chance to get right round the course,
show the world there is no need to doubt;
they spell it RISK, these cheery punters, full
of beans and home-made brew, all ready
for the unfrayed fray, the unfought fight, heady
with heavenly hope and bags of cotton wool
to shield their ears from earthy question marks.
They call this steeplechase the real McCoy,
ambrosia of every human ploy,
but when I strike the match it never sparks.

Life is fickle, leaves a gambling man
with odds and sods just trickling down the pan.

6 God

God must have thought it good,
shifting tectonic plates,
DNA mistakes,
and now those banks of food.

God must hope it's good,
all through those dreadful wars,
waiting at closed doors
for something understood.

God dreamed that it was good
to risk a human womb,
explore a human tomb,
do all God said God would.

Will everything turn out all right?
Part seven God will have to write.

Lonely Roads

Job chapter 28

Lonely the miner's path
digging for gold, digging for coal,
digging for some victory?
More like digging for survival.

Lonely the survivors walk:
children, sisters, brothers lost
– Aleppo, Aberfan, the Iolaire;
who adds up the human cost?

Lonely the philosopher
who lives uneasily inside us,
seeking at every pithead
shafts of light to guide us.

Jardins de la Tamarita

In Catalonia they seek pleasure and play
on the dusty floor of a botanic garden.

This is where the boys of Barcelona
measure lusty kickabouts against their dreams
of a professional future. As they say,
Barça is more than a football club.

Kike fingers his bansuri, watches his son
run on the hard ground. His melody repeats.
This scene is found, playing, all over Europe.

Margarida sits, finishes an ink sketch
of that gnarled clifftop eucalyptus, which
might be talking to the sky about the life
of every person walking, running down below.

In Catalonia they catch leisure, and lay
it down to flower in the human jungle.

Mungo's Legacy

Not your usual jaunt from East to West,
to Glasgow or to sainthood.
Thrown by royal Loth off Traprain's cliffs,
cast adrift to cross the Forth,
storing up a trauma in the womb
to occupy a lifetime's therapy,
Mungo birthed at Culross, and the rest
is history – or legend if you will.

They came back, Mungo's bairns; re-settled
post-war streets in Haddington,
where they could nod to Traprain's bulk,
choose their own voyages of life and love,
without benefit of monks or ministers,
play leapfrog with the memory of Knox,
play catch up with the country folk
who know the score, and name each hill.

Here SNP and Labour vie to throw
each other's yoke off, fight or argue for
that Holyrood control, the saintliness
or ugliness of power – while Glasgow
maybe still remembers Mungo, with
his godly therapy, his special words
to calm the storm and cross divides,
his goodness spite could never kill.

On the Square

Tangled rod ends dangle in their metal webs,
no longer able to conceal their reinforcement
of the hard core guts of money making
in this once rich square. High cranes take days
to launder work space, disengage blue cladding,
grab at rubbish concrete with their jagged jaws,
worrying it like a dog, dropping it in clouds
of dust controlled by well-aimed water sprays.

Such rough treatment of two million hours
of history . . . on his column, Viscount Melville
notices and gives an angry cough: first trams,
and now a shopping mall, what next, a helipad?
Is this the distant fruit of that enlightened brilliance
which propelled us to pan-European heights?
Or is it more the slow unpicking of Establishment,
so should we click at once on 'like', or be heart-sad?

The Square began with Dundas House, which soon became
the Royal Bank head office, with its hall and features
starring in some banknotes still in circulation.
The British Linen Bank was built upon its flanks
in 1806, and taken over by the Bank of Scotland.
The Union Bank (now RBS) then gobbled up
the National Bank; with a sense of *dèja vu* we ask,
'They regulate their clients . . . who regulates the banks?'

The famous lived there in the Square – Lord Henry
Brougham and David Hume, who hosted intellectual
dinner parties, probably without miraculous content.
He could not see arrive at number five a later

theist neighbour, National Bible Society, spreading
scriptures as the great philosopher once exported
his ideas. Today, instead of books and sparkling wine
and conversation, yawns a flat and empty crater.

Scottish Provident sold their Life Assurance first
in 1837. Their actuaries ruled like kings, and
one chipped daily golf balls from his office window
perfectly onto the grassy centre, till his status
changed from mild celebrity to minor criminal.
Spot on the Millennium, Abbey bought them over,
asset stripped them, took the loot to Glasgow
dodging history's question: 'Just how will they rate us?'

And where is old St Andrew in this pilgrimage of fame?
How does he match young Vincent Street and Charlotte Square,
with his chosen site gazumped by Melville's mansion?
Seems like money talks, and sainthood walks a furlong
further west to build a modest church in George Street.
On the demolition site, some railings shape a cross
held up on listed buildings pleading for survival,
while the Planners hold the key to right and wrong.

Dundas was 'on the square': at least he got the name
'Grand Manager of Scotland', or 'Ninth King Harry'.
Now labels cover all: this is a project shared
with Peveril Securities, though under Standard Life,
to turn the corridors of high finance into the lanes
between deodorant and toothpaste, with a nod
to history above – some office space, and at the top
the penthouse flats. Here is no sub-standard life.

Read the Signs

Jeremiah 32.6-12

A straight screw finds a pass
for Jeremiah's cousin Hanamel,
and a bolt snaps somewhere,

giving easy prison access
to a lawyer named Baruch.
Witnesses turn up on time.

The deed is signed – events
then take their crooked path
and creep or stride into our lives

with unexpected consequence
for good and ill, prophetic
elbows nudging us each day.

She fills in forms politely,
clicks them through a second time;
the migrants put down roots

in Babylon or Britain; still,
there's someone stubborn ploughing
hope into the ground back home.

A seed is carried in the flood,
buddlejas wave at passing trains,
fans still follow Cowdenbeath.

The bruised finger retrieves the ring,
distressed flats are clad again,
Americans keep going to the polls.

The boy puts down a stone, seeing
the ancient tree roots crack a wall;
somewhere a prophet buys a field.